An Extraordinary True Story of the American Revolution

Henry and the CANNONS

DON BROWN

ROARING BROOK PRESS NEW YORK

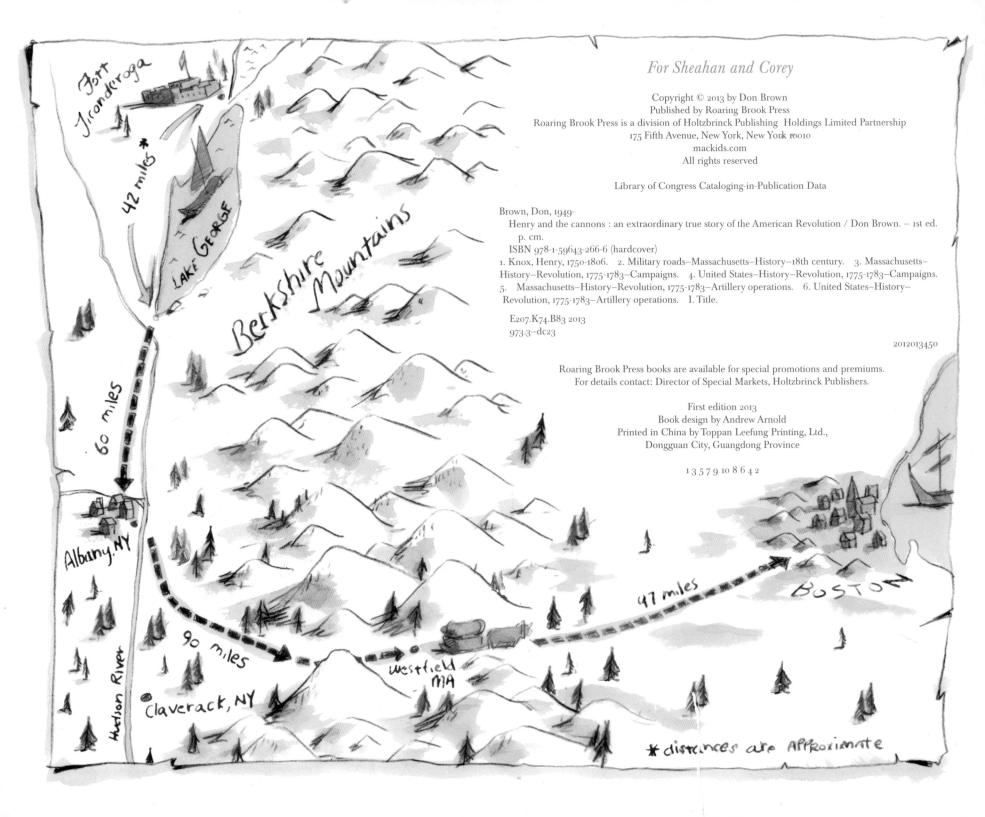

For Sheahan and Corey

Copyright © 2013 by Don Brown
Published by Roaring Brook Press
Roaring Brook Press is a division of Holtzbrinck Publishing Holdings Limited Partnership
175 Fifth Avenue, New York, New York 10010
mackids.com

Library of Congress Cataloging-in-Publication Data

Brown, Don, 1949-
   Henry and the cannons : an extraordinary true story of the American Revolution / Don Brown. — 1st ed.
   p. cm.
   ISBN 978-1-59643-266-6 (hardcover)
1. Knox, Henry, 1750-1806.   2. Military roads—Massachusetts—History—18th century.   3. Massachusetts—History—Revolution, 1775-1783—Campaigns.   4. United States—History—Revolution, 1775-1783—Campaigns.
5.   Massachusetts—History—Revolution, 1775-1783—Artillery operations.   6. United States—History—Revolution, 1775-1783—Artillery operations.   I. Title.

E207.K74.B83 2013
973.3—dc23
                                                                2012013450

Roaring Brook Press books are available for special promotions and premiums.
For details contact: Director of Special Markets, Holtzbrinck Publishers.

First edition 2013
Book design by Andrew Arnold
Printed in China by Toppan Leefung Printing, Ltd.,
Dongguan City, Guangdong Province

1 3 5 7 9 10 8 6 4 2

Fort Ticonderoga

42 miles *

Lake George

Berkshire Mountains

60 miles

Albany, NY

Hudson River

90 miles

Claverack, NY

Westfield MA

47 miles

BOSTON

* distances are approximate

It was the winter of 1775.

The American Revolution had begun,
and things weren't going well for the Patriots
of Boston, Massachusetts.

The British Army held the city. They thumbed their noses at the surrounding hills, where General George Washington and his soldiers stared down at them. The British and Washington both knew the modest American army had scant chance against the world's best soldiers.

Washington ached for cannons. With them,
he could rain cannonballs on the British soldiers' heads
and drive them from Boston.

But Washington had none.

At Fort Ticonderoga, New York, there were many cannons. In May, Colonel
Benedict Arnold had snatched the big guns, as well as the fort, from the British. But
300 miles of lakes and rivers, hills and glades, and mountain forests separated Boston
from Fort Ticonderoga.

Dragging the cannons the whole, hard way in winter was impossible.

Wasn't it?

Henry Knox said he could do it.

Knox was a Boston bookseller who'd taught himself soldiering from some of the very books he sold. In spite of a plump shape that suggested a man who preferred a good meal to a good fight, he was an eager Patriot who was sure he could bring the cannons to Boston.

General Washington believed
Henry and ordered him to Fort
Ticonderoga.

Covering forty miles a day
for a week of hard riding on
horseback, he was rain soaked,
windblown, and frozen. The trip
was nothing like selling books.

It would be the easiest part of
his adventure.

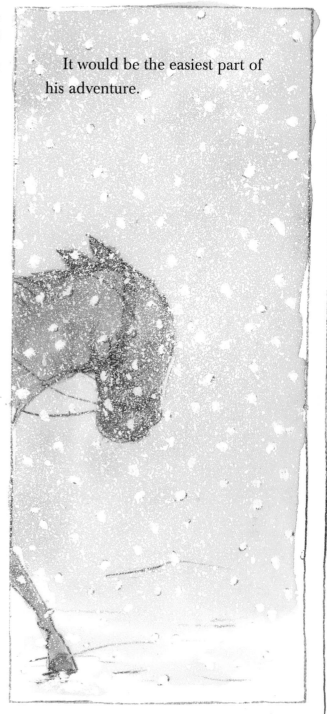

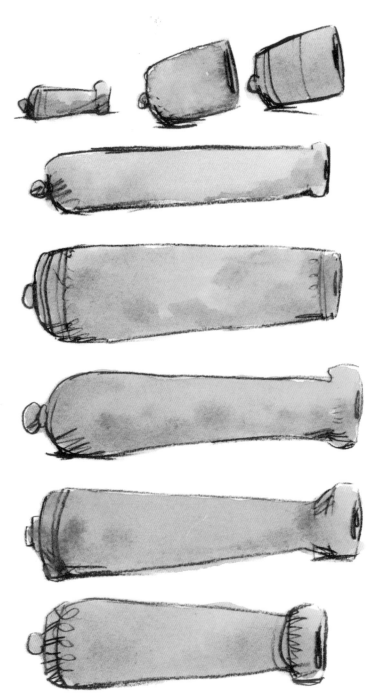

At the fort, Henry set about choosing
the best cannons.
Some big.
Some small.
120,000 pounds of cannon.
Fifty-nine in all.

He gathered men to help him on the journey back to Boston. First, they heaved the cannons to nearby Lake George where Henry had arranged for three boats to sail part of the way home.

Henry and his band set sail over icy waters.

Along the way, one boat snagged a rock. With ropes water-soaked and slick, the crew manhandled it free.

That night, Henry and his tired men found shelter with Native Americans. Henry declared their food "relishing."

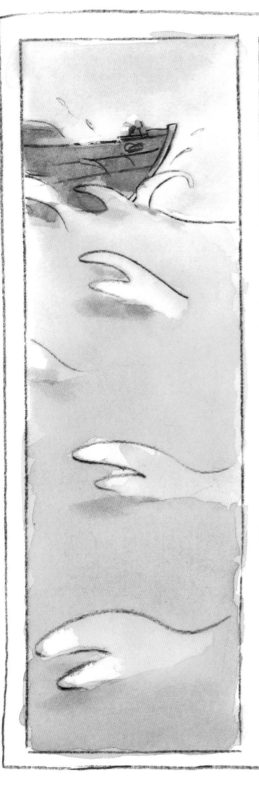

The next day, a wind sprang up "very fresh and directly against" the boats.

They had to be rowed hard for hours. Muscles and breath burned.

Wind-driven waves washed over the boats, sinking one.
Wet and cold, Henry's troop re-floated it.

After ten days and almost forty miles on the water, they reached the end of the lake.

Henry loaded the cannons onto forty-two sleds provided by local Patriots. Oxen and horses started hauling them over snowy roads. But the weather warmed and the snow disappeared. The sleds sank in the mud and stuck.

Certain the snow would return, Henry decided to scout the route ahead. He was alone and off the beaten path when a heavy storm blew in. Snow filled the air and piled high on the ground. His horse refused to go farther in the wintery gloom and deepening drifts. Henry trudged for miles before reaching safety.

"I had almost perished with the cold," he said.

But the sleds could be moved again.

The oxen and horses dragged them over frosty trails and across frozen rivers.

At one crossing, some cannons crashed through the ice into the water.

Henry refused to leave any cannon behind.
Pulling and tugging, lifting and yanking, hauling and lugging,
Henry's men rescued the drowned cannons.

The caravan had been struggling for about a month. They reached the Berkshire Mountains of Massachusetts and the road nearly disappeared. With shouts and cracking of whips, Henry and his band urged the straining oxen and horses forward.

In Boston, Washington watched British soldiers in their bright red uniforms marching Boston's streets, eating Boston's food, and sleeping in Boston's beds.

Using poles, ropes, and chains, Henry's men wrestled the cannons over the sheerest cliffs and down the steepest heights. Snow swam around their boots, and cold chilled their hands and faces, but no one quit.

On and on, Henry and his men trudged. Eventually, dizzying heights became steep slopes, then gentle hills, then a regular road and towns appeared again.

Many of the townspeople had never seen a cannon.

In Westfield, Massachusetts, Henry fired a big gun and thrilled everyone.

Finally, about fifty days after leaving Fort Ticonderoga,
Henry reached General Washington outside Boston.
Not a single cannon had been lost.

Nearly three months later, 2,000 Americans scrambled up the hills overlooking Boston in the dark of night. With 300 oxcarts and wagons, they hauled wood and barrels to make a fortress for Knox's cannons.

They finished by dawn, the daylight revealing a nasty surprise for the British.

Seeing the big guns pointing down at them, the 9,000 British soldiers fled the city by boat. They left behind 250 of their own cannons.

The Americans won back their city and a great victory.

It was March 17, 1776. George Washington led a joyful parade into Boston.

Beside him was Henry.

Bibliography

Callahan, North. *Henry Knox: George Washington's General.* New York: Rinehart & Co., 1958.

Kirschbaum, Joseph W. and Autum Resney. *Military History* 19, no. 5 (Dec. 2002): 24.

Langguth, A. J. *Patriots: The Men Who Started the American Revolution.* New York: Simon and Shuster, 1989.

Middlekauff, Robert. *The Glorious Cause: The American Revolution, 1763–1789.* New York: Oxford University Press, 1982.

Puls, Mark. *Henry Knox: Visionary General of the American Revolution.* New York: Palgrave Macmillan, 2008.

The Knox Trail–History. A New York State History Month 2000 Project. www.nysm.nysed.gov/services/KnoxTrail/kthistory